Mystery history of the
TROJAN
HORSE

Jim Pipe

COPPER BEECH BOOKS
BROOKFIELD, CONNECTICUT

© Aladdin Books Ltd 1997
© U.S. text 1997

Designed and produced by
Aladdin Books Ltd
28 Percy Street
London W1P 0LD

*First published in
the United States in 1997 by*
Copper Beech Books,
an imprint of
The Millbrook Press
2 Old New Milford Road
Brookfield, Connecticut 06804

Consultant
Peter Derow
Editor
Jon Richards
Designed by
David West Children's Book
Design
Designer
Simon Morse
Illustrated by
Roger Hutchins
Donald Harley –
B.L. Kearley Ltd
Additional illustrations by
David Burroughs
Rob Shone

Printed in Belgium

**Library of Congress
Cataloging-in-Publication Data**

Pipe, Jim, 1966-
Trojan horse / Jim Pipe ; illustrated by
Roger Hutchins and Donald Hartley.
p. cm. — (Mystery history of a—)
Includes index.
ISBN 0-7613-0626-9 (trade hardcover).
— ISBN 0-7613-0614-5 (lib. bdg.)
1. Greece—Civilization—To 146 B.C.
—Juvenile literature.
2. Cities and towns, Ancient—Greece
—Juvenile literature.
I. Title II. Series: Mystery history.
DF78.P6 1997   97-10021
938—dc21   CIP

Contents

The Trojan Horse

This book looks at the history of ancient Greece from the Trojan Wars (about 1250 B.C.) to the campaigns of Alexander the Great in the 4th century B.C. It shows how the remarkable Greek people were inspired and influenced by the legends of the past – in particular by the story of the capture of Troy with a wooden horse (*above*).

In about 750 B.C., these legends were written down by Homer in his epic poems the *Iliad* and the *Odyssey*. To the ancient Greeks, these tales were not myth, but history. Their religion was based on the gods Homer described, their nobles claimed his heroes were their forefathers, and children were taught using his poems. So read on and discover the mysterious world of the Greeks (*see* map *right*) where myth and reality can be hard to separate!

The Mystery of History

Though we can learn about Greece from surviving books and objects (like this Mycenaean death mask, *above*), there's still a lot that we don't know. So as you read, try to imagine the sights, sounds, and smells of Greece. Who knows, your guess might be right. That's the real mystery of history!

USING MYSTERY HISTORY

You'll find that *Mystery History of the Trojan Horse* is packed with puzzles and mysteries for you to solve. But before you go any further, read the instructions below to get the most out of the book!

Hunt the Spy

One of the characters in the book is a Spartan spy! No one knows who, but on page 29, some likely suspects have been lined up.

To help you work out which one of them is on a secret mission, clues are given in six Hunt the Spy *boxes. If you answer the questions correctly,* the clues will help you to work out what the spy looks like, for example, hair color. But to get the right answers you will need to read the book carefully. Happy hunting!

Pythagoras' Puzzles

The sign of the horse marks a special puzzle that can be anything from a maze to a secret Greek code. Answers for these puzzles are given in The Oracle Answers.

True or False?

Some pages have a teasing True or False *question with an answer (on page 29) that may surprise you!*

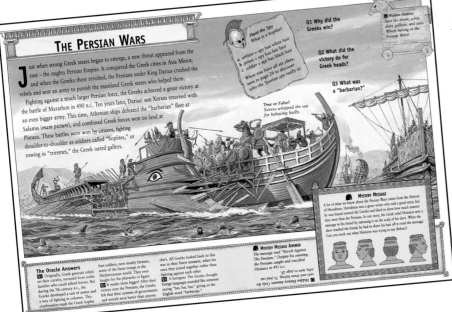

THE PERSIAN WARS

Just when strong Greek states began to emerge, a new threat appeared from the east – the mighty Persian Empire. It conquered the Greek cities in Asia Minor, and when the Greeks there revolted, the Persians under King Darius crushed the rebels and sent an army to punish the mainland Greek states who helped them. Fighting against a much larger Persian force, the Greeks achieved a great victory at the battle of Marathon in 490 B.C. Ten years later, Darius' son Xerxes returned with an even bigger army. This time, Athenian ships defeated the "barbarian" fleet at Salamis (*main picture*), and combined Greek forces won on land at Plataea. These battles were won by citizens, fighting shoulder-to-shoulder as soldiers called "hoplites," or rowing in "triremes," the Greek oared galleys.

Hunt the Spy What is a hoplite?
a athlete = spy has white hair
b priest = spy has fair hair
c soldier = spy has black hair
When you have all six clues, turn to page 29 to discover who the Spartan spy really is!

Q1 Why did the Greeks win?

Q2 What did the victory do for Greek heads?

Q3 What was a "barbarian?"

True or False? Xerxes whipped the sea for behaving badly.

Hidden History Spot the drum, whip, diver, galleon, and sails. Which belong in the Persian Wars?

MYSTERY MESSAGE
A lot of what we know about the Persian Wars comes from the *History* of Herodotus. Herodotus was a great writer who told a good story, but he was biased toward the Greeks and liked to show how much smarter they were than the Persians. In one story, the Greek rebel Histiaios sent a message to his friend by tattooing it on the scalp of his slave. When the slave reached the friend, he had to shave his hair off to read the message. Can you work out what Histiaios was trying to say (below)?

MYSTERY MESSAGE ANSWER
The message read "Revolt Against The Persians." Despite his cunning, the Persians caught and crucified Histiaios in 493 B.C.

Hidden History Answer: Only the whip, drum, and sails belong. The first submarine was invented in 1620.

The Oracle Answers
Q1 Originally, Greek generals relied on their cavalry, recruited from noble families who could afford horses. But during the 7th century B.C., the Greeks developed a suit of armor and a way of fighting in columns. This combination made the Greek hoplite foot soldiers, now mostly farmers, some of the finest troops in the Mediterranean world. They even fought for the pharaohs in Egypt. **Q2** It makes them bigger! After their victory over the Persians, the Greeks felt that their systems of governments and morals were better than anyone else's. All Greeks looked back to this war as their finest moment, when for once they joined together rather than fighting against each other. **Q3** A foreigner. The Greeks thought foreign languages sounded like someone saying "bar, bar, bar," giving us the English word "barbarian."

Hidden History

Hidden History Can you spot Merlin, Pegasus, a dragon, the giant cyclops, an Amazon, and the goddess Athena. Which don't belong in Greek myth?

Try to find the objects that are cleverly hidden in the artwork, then guess if you would really see them in ancient Greece.

History Mysteries

Dotted around the page are questions like: **Q2 Does anyone cheat at the Olympic games?** *Try to think about these before reading the answer in* The Oracle Answers.

The Oracle Answers

Answers to Hidden History 🅀, *the History Mysteries* **Q1**, *and Pythagoras' Puzzles* 🐴 *are given in this panel at the bottom of each page.*

The Legend of the Horse

At the back of the book are full answers to Hidden History *and* True or False, *a lineup of suspects (one of whom is the Spartan spy), and, last but not least, a fantastic aerial view of ancient Troy as the Greeks imagined it that also has some exciting puzzles (right)!*

THE LEGEND OF TROY

It all started when the Trojan prince Paris persuaded Helen, the wife of a Greek king, to run away with him to Troy. The Greeks were furious, and under King Agamemnon a fleet of a thousand ships sailed to Troy. The Greeks besieged the city for ten years before Odysseus thought of making a giant wooden horse, in which a few soldiers could hide. The horse was left outside Troy while the Greeks pretended to sail away. The Trojans foolishly dragged the horse inside the walls. When night came, the hidden warriors crept out and opened the city gates for the waiting Greek Army. Troy was burned to the ground, and the legend had begun... This is the story as the Greeks told it – a tale that was to inspire them for hundreds of years.

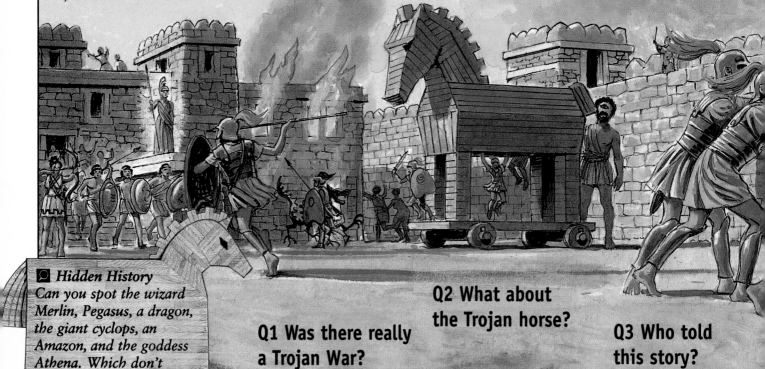

Hidden History
Can you spot the wizard Merlin, Pegasus, a dragon, the giant cyclops, an Amazon, and the goddess Athena. Which don't belong in Greek myth?

Q1 Was there really a Trojan War?

Q2 What about the Trojan horse?

Q3 Who told this story?

The Oracle Answers

Q1 Perhaps. Many historians believe that the story of the Trojan War, like many Greek legends, refers to an event that really happened. But like all stories, especially ones that aren't written down at the time, the details become more and more incredible.

It wasn't unusual for raiders to carry off rival queens, but the war was probably about trade. Ancient Troy was in an ideal place (*see* map, page 2) to control the flow of gold, timber, spices, and linen from the Black Sea, and the Greeks would have wanted control of these goods. The war may have lasted ten years, but was perhaps a series of small raids rather than one long siege.

Hidden History Answer: Only Merlin belongs. To find out why, turn to page 28.

THE TROJAN MYSTERY

In 1870 the German archaeologist Heinrich Schliemann (1822–1890, *left*), inspired by the stories of the Trojan War in Homer's *Iliad*, decided to search for the lost city.

Remarkably, he found not one city but nine, buried beneath a huge mound at Hisarlik in Turkey. Each city stood on the ruins of the one before it. Of the nine, Troy VIIa is probably the most likely city of the story as it was destroyed by fire in 1250 B.C. Near the bottom of the mound, Schliemann found many splendid treasures, such as gold jewelry, silver goblets, and vases.

The Pottery Puzzle

Schliemann claimed the jewels belonged to Priam, the mythical king of Troy, but archaeologists now believe that they came from an earlier city built a thousand years before the war. Moreover, Troy VIIa was not full of splendid palaces – in fact its inhabitants lived in poor, badly made houses. So what happened to the Troy in the story? Perhaps we will never know.

Imagine you are sifting through pieces of broken pottery in the lost city of Troy (*right*). Which of the pieces a-d (*above*) will complete the pot?

Q2 There are many explanations for the horse: e.g. perhaps the Greeks used cavalry to defeat the Trojans.

But maybe this part of the story has more to do with the fact that the ancient Greeks thought they were smarter than everyone else, and liked to hear this tale of Greek cunning.

Q3 The original storytellers were bards, traveling poets and musicians who sang epic stories of ancient heroes. Like today's rappers, they used familiar rhymes and set phrases to help keep their stories going. But in about 750 B.C., Homer, a Greek writer from Ionia (the region near Troy), wrote down the stories in two poems called the *Iliad* and the *Odyssey*. These can still be read today.

TROJAN MYSTERY ANSWER

Only piece d fits. Pieces a and c are the wrong shape, and piece b gives the horse figure an octopus head!

THE PALACE AT KNOSSOS

Q1 What were the Minoans like?

Q2 What goes on in the palace?

Q3 How are the Minoans linked to the Trojan War?

True or False?
The ancient Cretans used goats to pull their chariots.

◎ Hidden History
Can you spot the soccer ball, kangaroo, matador, and Minotaur? Which don't belong in the myths of ancient Crete?

◎ *Hidden History Answer: Only the Minotaur belongs.*
To find out the reasons why, turn to page 28.

The Oracle Answers

Q1 The Minoans were very organized and kept records on clay tablets. These show that their king was helped by a large staff, run by a sort of chief minister. The tablets also show a wide range of trades, from shepherds and metalworkers to shipbuilders and bakers. The Cretans were very artistic.

They painted their walls with beautiful scenes of everyday life and produced fine jewelry, carvings, and pottery. They also liked to live in luxury: They had marble baths and toilets flushed by streams!

Q2 Traditionally, Knossos was thought to be the king's palace, but it may have also been a temple, where the incredible sport of

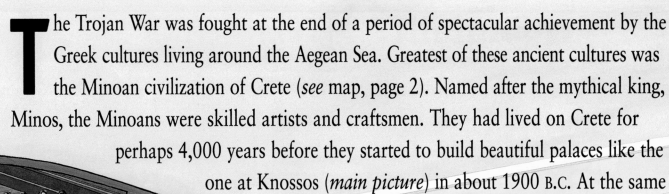

The Trojan War was fought at the end of a period of spectacular achievement by the Greek cultures living around the Aegean Sea. Greatest of these ancient cultures was the Minoan civilization of Crete (*see* map, page 2). Named after the mythical king, Minos, the Minoans were skilled artists and craftsmen. They had lived on Crete for perhaps 4,000 years before they started to build beautiful palaces like the one at Knossos (*main picture*) in about 1900 B.C. At the same time, they set up trading posts in the islands of the Aegean Sea and in Egypt, and their power spread across Greece. By 1405 B.C., however, the Minoans were in trouble. First, a volcano erupted on the nearby island of Thera, ruining their harvest with clouds of dust. Then a series of earthquakes hit Crete, destroying the great palaces at Mallia and Zakro.

bull jumping, the double-headed axes, and the snake goddess (can you spot all these?) were linked together in a mysterious Cretan religion.

Q3 One explanation for the Trojan War is that after the collapse of the powerful Minoan culture, other peoples, such as the mainland Greeks and Trojans, were left to fight over trade routes once dominated by the Minoans.

THE LABYRINTH PUZZLE

The story of Theseus may be based on history. In the legend, King Minos builds a huge maze, the labyrinth, as a home for a half-man, half-bull monster, the Minotaur. The beast feeds on young Athenians sent every year to Crete as tribute, until the Greek hero Theseus finally kills it.

Some historians believe this describes a revolt by Athenians against their Cretan masters. The palace at Knossos, with its many corridors and different levels, is certainly a bit like a maze. Perhaps the legend also hints at a dark secret of human sacrifice! Can you find your way out of this maze, starting from the center, by the bull's head (*left*)?

THE MIGHTY MYCENAEANS

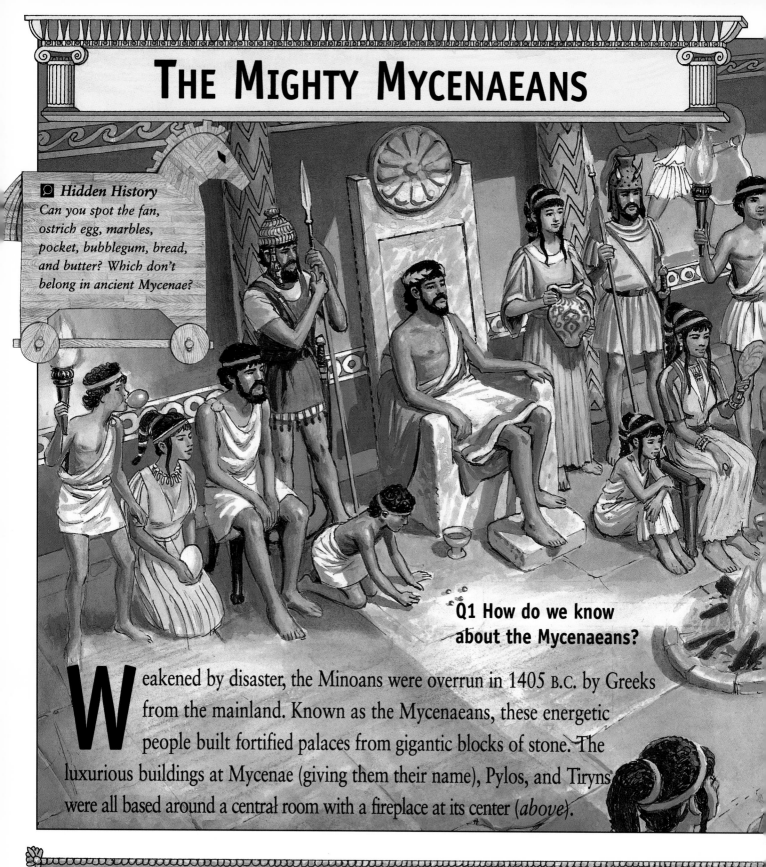

Hidden History
Can you spot the fan, ostrich egg, marbles, pocket, bubblegum, bread, and butter? Which don't belong in ancient Mycenae?

Q1 How do we know about the Mycenaeans?

Weakened by disaster, the Minoans were overrun in 1405 B.C. by Greeks from the mainland. Known as the Mycenaeans, these energetic people built fortified palaces from gigantic blocks of stone. The luxurious buildings at Mycenae (giving them their name), Pylos, and Tiryns were all based around a central room with a fireplace at its center (*above*).

THE ORACLE ANSWERS

Q1 We know a lot from graves discovered at Mycenae and Pylos. The Mycenaeans took death very seriously, and, as well as placing many fine objects in the graves of the rich, they pickled their bodies in honey!

The stone vases and bronze boxes found in the 16th-century-B.C tombs reveal the Mycenaeans' busy trading, while beautiful cups and daggers show their great wealth and artistry.

Perhaps the most exciting finds were the golden death masks (*see* page 2), a symbol of a Mycenaean king's immortality. Heinrich Schliemann, the same man who discovered Troy, claimed that one mask belonged to King Agamemnon, legendary leader of the Greeks at Troy!

Hidden History Answers: *The bubblegum, pocket, and butter don't belong!* *Turn to page 28 to find out why.*

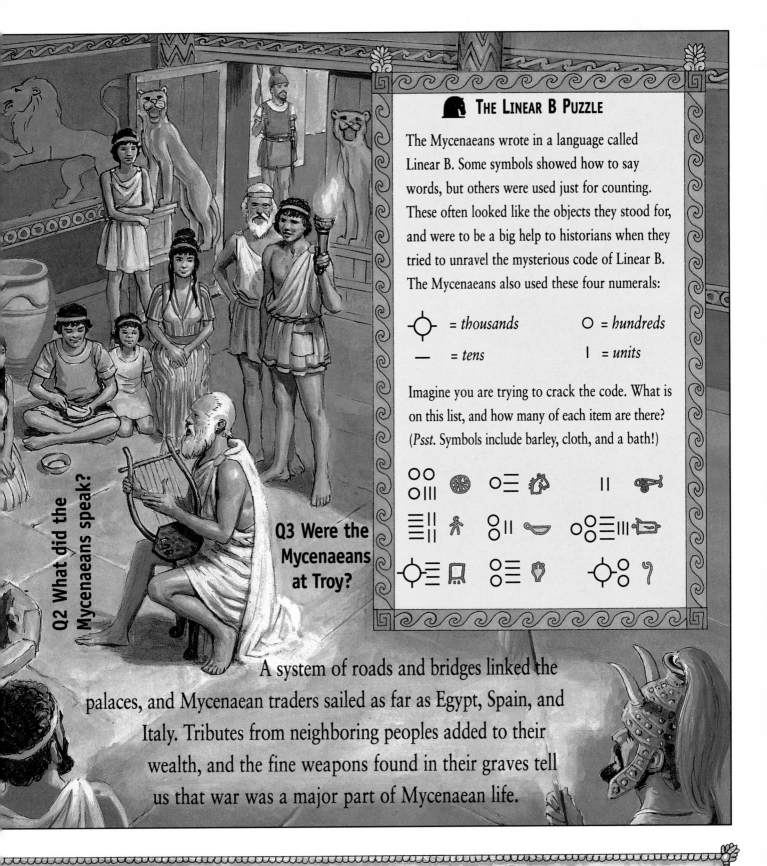

THE LINEAR B PUZZLE

The Mycenaeans wrote in a language called Linear B. Some symbols showed how to say words, but others were used just for counting. These often looked like the objects they stood for, and were to be a big help to historians when they tried to unravel the mysterious code of Linear B. The Mycenaeans also used these four numerals:

⊕ = *thousands*   ○ = *hundreds*

— = *tens* | = *units*

Imagine you are trying to crack the code. What is on this list, and how many of each item are there? (*Psst.* Symbols include barley, cloth, and a bath!)

Q2 What did the Mycenaeans speak?

Q3 Were the Mycenaeans at Troy?

A system of roads and bridges linked the palaces, and Mycenaean traders sailed as far as Egypt, Spain, and Italy. Tributes from neighboring peoples added to their wealth, and the fine weapons found in their graves tell us that war was a major part of Mycenaean life.

Q2 Though their writing was probably borrowed from the Minoans of Crete, the language spoken by the Mycenaeans was definitely an early form of Greek. By the 8th century B.C., the fact that all Greeks spoke pretty much the same language made them feel they were somehow special.

Q3 Homer may have based part of the *Iliad* on old tales about the Mycenaeans. Many of the details in his poems, however, do not fit the archaeological evidence found at Mycenae. Though Agamemnon was later worshipped at Mycenae, we have no proof that he ever existed.

LINEAR B PUZZLE ANSWER

Left column – 303 wheels, 54 slaves, and 1,040 lengths of cloth. Middle column – 130 horses, 202 cups, and 240 vases. Right column – 2 chariots, 343 baths, and 1,200 measures of barley. If you got these right, perhaps you should become an archaeologist!

THE DARK AGE

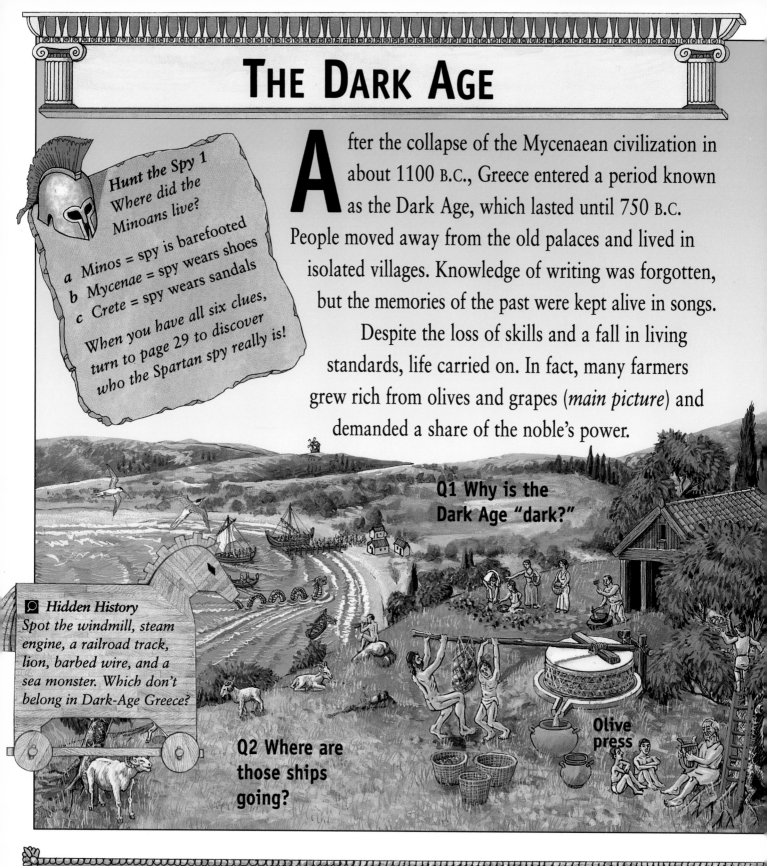

After the collapse of the Mycenaean civilization in about 1100 B.C., Greece entered a period known as the Dark Age, which lasted until 750 B.C. People moved away from the old palaces and lived in isolated villages. Knowledge of writing was forgotten, but the memories of the past were kept alive in songs. Despite the loss of skills and a fall in living standards, life carried on. In fact, many farmers grew rich from olives and grapes (*main picture*) and demanded a share of the noble's power.

Hunt the Spy 1
Where did the Minoans live?

a Minos = spy is barefooted
b Mycenae = spy wears shoes
c Crete = spy wears sandals

When you have all six clues, turn to page 29 to discover who the Spartan spy really is!

Hidden History
Spot the windmill, steam engine, a railroad track, lion, barbed wire, and a sea monster. Which don't belong in Dark-Age Greece?

Q1 Why is the Dark Age "dark?"

Q2 Where are those ships going?

Olive press

The Oracle Answers

Q1 The Dark Age is "dark" because no one writes anything down, so it is difficult to see what happened.

We know that Dorian invaders arrived from the north and forced many Greeks to flee to Asia Minor. Myths also suggest that the Mycenaeans fought among themselves. Whatever the cause, by the 8th century B.C. a new culture had appeared with iron weapons and a new style of pottery.

Q2 A rise in population may have encouraged many Greeks to leave the mainland in search of a hew home. New towns were built in Spain, Italy, France, North Africa, around the Black Sea, and even at Troy. Homer's poem the *Odyssey* may be partly based on sailor's wild tales from this period.

Hidden History Answer:
Only the lion belongs. To find out the reasons why, turn to page 28.

Without the security of the old palaces, which were now in ruins (*main picture*), the local nobles who had held onto power since Mycenaean times now looked to myth to justify their position. Many claimed that the legendary heroes of the Trojan War were their ancestors.

Q3 Why don't the farmers and nobles get along?

Grape crushing

🐴 HOMER'S PUZZLE

Homer's two great poems, the *Iliad* and the *Odyssey*, were based on folk tales that were 500 years old. When he wrote down his story, Homer used the set phrases of the old storytellers. For example, when he is talking about the dawn, Homer often used it with the phrase "rosy-fingered" to describe the red sky at this time of day. These Homeric phrases (*below*) have been mixed up. Can you match the right noun with the right adjective?

• *White-tusked*	Athena
• *Broad-shouldered*	ships
• *Long-oared*	Odysseus
• *Bright-eyed*	boars
• *Noisy*	lyres
• *Tuneful*	dogs

Q3 During the Dark Ages, farmers learned better methods of farming, especially with olive trees. They had always worked together, so it was natural for them to join together in a community, called a *polis*. They disliked the selfish heroic ideals of the past and took pride in their community. The rich nobles, however, still owned large areas of land and stayed wealthy by breeding horses. They preferred to work with rich people in other areas, rather than with everyone else in the community.

During the 7th and 6th centuries B.C., the farmers often supported a single leader, called a "tyrant," who tried to force the nobles out of power.

🐴 HOMER'S PUZZLE ANSWER

The correct answers are: bright-eyed Athena; long-oared ships; broad-shouldered Odysseus; white-tusked boars; tuneful lyres; and noisy dogs!

THE OLYMPIC GAMES

In the 8th century B.C., the Greek world rediscovered its energy. Borrowing the idea of an alphabet from the Phoenicians of Syria, the Greeks learned to write again. Painting, sculpture, and architecture also flourished. But perhaps the greatest symbol of this rebirth was the Olympic Games, first held in 776 B.C. at Olympia. Here, on sacred ground, athletes competed in a variety of games to honor the gods.

Q1 Why were the Olympics so special?

Q2 Was there any cheating?

Hidden History
Can you spot the torch, running shorts, piggyback fight, and soccer referee? Which don't belong in ancient Olympia?

The Oracle Answers

Q1 The games were much more than a sporting event. They were a celebration of what it was to be Greek. The games were also a highly religious occasion, held together with a festival to Olympian Zeus (whose ivory and gold statue was one of the seven wonders of the world).

Three heralds were sent to all the Greek states to announce the dates and to declare a truce. Fighting all over Greece stopped for a week and no arms were allowed at the games.

Poets also sang about the past, remembering events like the Trojan War, when the Greeks last combined to defeat a common enemy. Only Greek men and boys were allowed to take part (though foreigners could watch).

Hidden History Answer: The running shorts and referee don't belong. *To find out why, turn to page 28.*

Athletic festivals had been around long before the Olympics, as part of funeral rituals and as a focus for tribes or towns. But people came to Olympia (*left*) from far and wide – even from towns in Italy and North Africa. Here they joined fellow Greeks to worship their ancestors and to hear glorious tales of days gone by. Rich men used the games to show off their wealth and relive the heroic acts of their forefathers at Troy by competing in chariot races.

Q3 What events were there?

True or False?
Women could win some events.

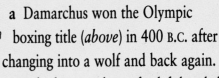

SUPERSTITION PUZZLE

The Greeks were a very superstitious people, and often confused real events, mythology, and the supernatural. Which of the following stories did they believe in?

a Damarchus won the Olympic boxing title (*above*) in 400 B.C. after changing into a wolf and back again.

b You had to watch out for left-handed people (*left*) as they were very strange.

c Olympic champions were half-god supermen whose statues could work miracles.

d Spirits, or daimons (*right*), helped you through life.

e The guts of dead animals could tell you the future.

Q2 Oh yes! The games started off as a contest between amateurs, but by the 6th century B.C. many competitors were sponsored by their *polis*. Winners were treated like gods, so cheating and bribing were common. Convicted cheats were forced to pay for statues.
Q3 The original games were a one-day event with a single footrace. By 500 B.C., the games lasted for three days, with foot, chariot, and horse races, boxing, and a bloody form of wrestling, *pankration* (using anything but teeth).

SUPERSTITION PUZZLE ANSWER
All of them! Even the philosopher Socrates (see page 22) believed his personal daimon protected him.

THE LAND OF THE GODS

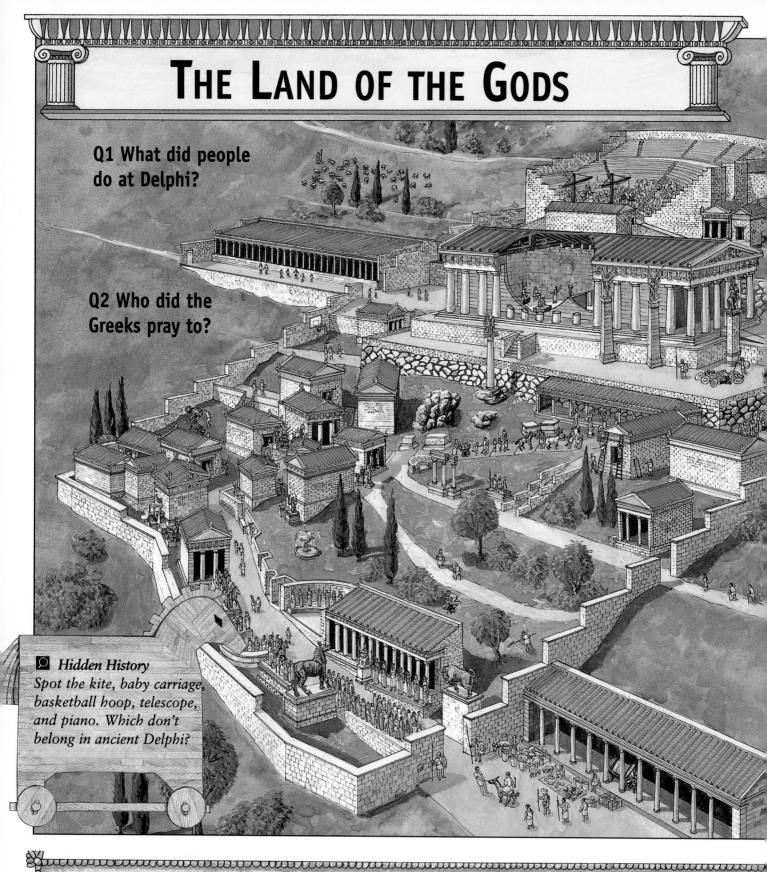

Q1 What did people do at Delphi?

Q2 Who did the Greeks pray to?

◉ *Hidden History*
Spot the kite, baby carriage, basketball hoop, telescope, and piano. Which don't belong in ancient Delphi?

The Oracle Answers

Q1 Most left behind gifts for the gods to win their favor. Individuals left behind small statuettes of animals or humans (such as shepherds or warriors), while states built large buildings to store all kinds of gold, silver, and other precious objects, like statues, vases, and shields.

The sacrifice of domestic animals, such as goats, was also an important part of worship. Different gods and goddesses needed different animals on specific days of the month. Special calendars were drawn up to show people when to sacrifice what. Feasts, poetry competitions, and games were often linked with religious festivals, and many sanctuaries had running tracks and theaters built near them.

◉ *Hidden History Answer:*
None of these things belong. To find out why, turn to page 28.

out why, turn to page 28.

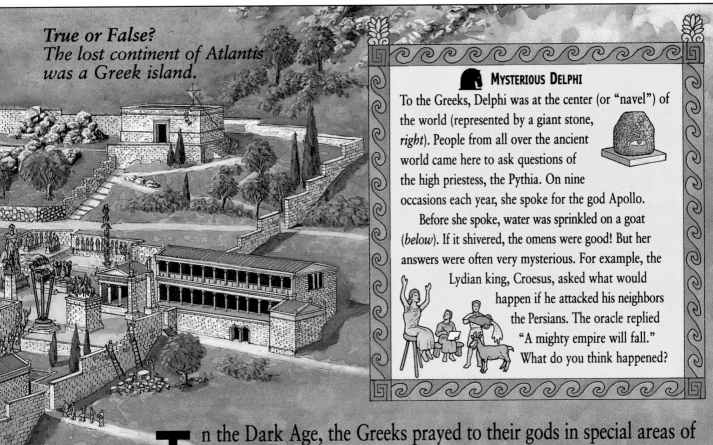

True or False?
The lost continent of Atlantis was a Greek island.

MYSTERIOUS DELPHI

To the Greeks, Delphi was at the center (or "navel") of the world (represented by a giant stone, *right*). People from all over the ancient world came here to ask questions of the high priestess, the Pythia. On nine occasions each year, she spoke for the god Apollo.

Before she spoke, water was sprinkled on a goat (*below*). If it shivered, the omens were good! But her answers were often very mysterious. For example, the Lydian king, Croesus, asked what would happen if he attacked his neighbors the Persians. The oracle replied "A mighty empire will fall." What do you think happened?

In the Dark Age, the Greeks prayed to their gods in special areas of sacred ground, bringing animals for sacrifice on simple altars. But from the 7th century B.C. onward, they started to build magnificent temples for their gods, such as the Parthenon that still stands on the Acropolis at Athens.

To the ancient Greeks, religion meant taking part in public festivals, saying prayers, pouring wine over family altars (*see* page 11), and visiting oracles at holy sites like Delphi (*main picture*). Every big occasion in their life was marked by a religious ceremony. The Greeks believed that in return for their offerings, the gods or spirits of their ancestors would give them the power to get what they wanted.

Hunt the Spy 2
Who is the goddess of the moon?

a Artemis = spy wears a colored tunic or robe

b Apollo = spy wears a white tunic or robe

c Athena = spy has no tunic

Collect the clues to discover who the Spartan spy really is!

Q2 The Greek religion was similar to the gods that appeared in Homer's poems. The twelve Homeric gods and goddesses that the Greeks prayed to were: Zeus, thundering king of the gods; Poseidon, god of the sea; Apollo, god of the sun; Artemis, goddess of the moon; Dionysus, god of ecstasy; Hermes, the messenger god; Athena, goddess of wisdom; Hephaestus, the blacksmith god; Ares, god of war; Demeter, the harvest goddess; Aphrodite, goddess of love; and Hera, queen of the gods. The gods were thought to live on Mount Olympus in central Greece.

MYSTERIOUS DELPHI

Croesus attacked and was defeated! When he complained, the oracle said he should have thought about which kingdom was going to fall.

THE TOUGH SPARTANS

By about 600 B.C., the scattered villages of Dark-Age Greece had slowly formed into states. Most were ruled by a council of "oligarchs," unelected wealthy men, or tyrants – strong leaders who ruled alone. However, the greatest Greek state of the age, Sparta, was ruled by two kings, who claimed they were descended from the demigod Heracles. They were helped by a council of old men, called the "gerousia." The Spartans believed that the state came first – and individual people second.

Hidden History
Spot the cake, camera, party dress, deodorant spray, and skateboard. Which don't belong in ancient Sparta?

Q1 So, was everyone terrified of the Spartans?

SPARTAN RULE PUZZLE

The Spartans lived according to a very strict set of rules. Which of the following do you think were part of the real Spartan code?

a Smile even if your brother is killed.
b Learn to steal food, including holy food from temples.
c Laugh at and bully those weaker than you.
d Sleep in warm rooms on a nice soft bed.
e Live on black broth – pork juices mixed with salt and vinegar into a soup (below).
f Never take prisoners.
g Have as many baths as you can.
h Boys, grow your hair as long as possible and comb it regularly.

The Oracle Answers
Q1 Yes and No. The Spartans were so confident about their army that they didn't bother to build walls around their city. Their discipline did allow them to fight brilliantly together, but because they were so worried about a helot (slave) revolt, they never let their army travel too far from home.

Hidden History Answer: None of these things belong. To find out why, *turn to page 28.*

Because of this, the Spartan lifestyle was very extreme. Sparta used its conquered peoples, called "helots," to farm the land as slaves, so that Spartan men could concentrate on being soldiers. Sparta was admired for its invincible army, and dominated the whole of the southern Greek peninsula, called the Peloponnese.

Hunt the Spy 3
Which Greek god or goddess is linked to the oracle at Delphi?

a Pythia = spy is short
b Apollo = spy is tall
c Zeus = spy is medium height

Turn to page 29 when you have collected all six clues!

Q2 Was it fun being a Spartan?

True or False?
The Spartan army was led by an animal.

Q2 Not really. The Spartans prided themselves on brute strength, courage, and talking straight. At birth, the council of elders, the gerousia, decided whether a child was strong enough. "Weak" babies were left to die in the mountains. Boys left home at 7 to be trained as warriors. At 20, they were full citizens, but still lived with their fellow soldiers even if they were married. Girls were also taught to wrestle and throw spears. Even Spartan religion was tough. In one festival, a boy was whipped until he fainted, in another, gangs of boys beat each other up to encourage a feeling of community.

SPARTAN RULE PUZZLE ANSWER
Rules d and g are false. The Spartans lived in cold, damp rooms with only rushes to sleep on. They also thought washing was for wimps – most Spartans only had a bath a few times every year – no wonder their enemies always ran away from them in battle!

THE PERSIAN WARS

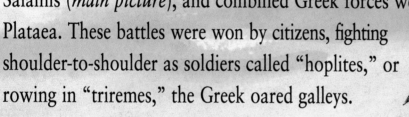

Just when strong Greek states began to emerge, a new threat appeared from the east – the mighty Persian Empire. It conquered the Greek cities in Asia Minor, and when the Greeks there revolted, the Persians under King Darius crushed the rebels and sent an army to punish the mainland Greek states who helped them.

Fighting against a much larger Persian force, the Greeks achieved a great victory at the battle of Marathon in 490 B.C. Ten years later, Darius' son Xerxes returned with an even bigger army. This time, Athenian ships defeated the "barbarian" fleet at Salamis (*main picture*), and combined Greek forces won on land at Plataea. These battles were won by citizens, fighting shoulder-to-shoulder as soldiers called "hoplites," or rowing in "triremes," the Greek oared galleys.

The Oracle Answers

Q1 Originally, Greek generals relied on their cavalry, recruited from noble families who could afford horses. But during the 7th century B.C., the Greeks developed a suit of armor and a way of fighting in columns. This combination made the Greek hoplite foot soldiers, now mostly farmers, some of the finest troops in the Mediterranean world. They even fought for the pharaohs in Egypt.

Q2 It mades them bigger! After their victory over the Persians, the Greeks felt that their systems of governments and morals were better than anyone else's. All Greeks looked back to this war as their finest moment, when for once they joined together rather than fighting against each other.

Q3 A foreigner. The Greeks thought foreign languages sounded like someone saying "bar, bar, bar," giving us the English word "barbarian."

Hunt the Spy
What is a hoplite?

a athlete = spy has white hair
b priest = spy has fair hair
c soldier = spy has black hair

When you have all six clues, turn to page 29 to discover who the Spartan spy really is!

Q1 Why did the Greeks win?

Q2 What did the victory do for Greek heads?

Q3 What was a "barbarian?"

Hidden History
Spot the drum, whip, diver, galleon, and sails. Which belong in the Persian Wars?

True or False?
Xerxes whipped the sea for behaving badly.

MYSTERY MESSAGE

A lot of what we know about the Persian Wars comes from the *History* of Herodotus. Herodotus was a great writer who told a good story, but he was biased toward the Greeks and liked to show how much smarter they were than the Persians. In one story, the Greek rebel Histiaios sent a message to his friend by tattooing it on the scalp of his slave. When the slave reached the friend, he had to shave his hair off to read the message. Can you work out what Histiaios was trying to say (*below*)?

SIANSRE   HEPER   VOLTAG   AINSTT

MYSTERY MESSAGE ANSWER
The message read "Revolt Against The Persians." Despite his cunning, the Persians caught and crucified Histiaios in 493 B.C.

Hidden History Answer: Only the sails and drum belong. To find out why, turn to page 28.

THE ATHENIAN ASSEMBLY

The cooperation between the Greek states did not last long after the Persian Wars. Soon the Spartans and Athenians set about building rival empires. In Sparta, the kings remained in power, and most other states were still ruled by the rich. In 5th-century-B.C. Athens, however, there was a revolutionary new type of government. For the first time, the farmers who had fought the Persians and the poor who crewed the ships could take part in decision-making.

Q1 What happened in the Assembly?

Q2 Did everyone take part?

The Oracle Answers

Q1 Imagine a government where every day, anyone can turn up to vote! Some 6,000 men from a population of 40,000 males could fit into the Pnyx, the open-air meeting place of the Assembly. With so many people, votes were taken not by a count, but by a show of hands in the air.

The Assembly was a religious event, but things could get very rowdy. Everyone had the right to speak, but could only speak for a set time. If you spoke for too long, you could be dragged off the stand (*see main picture*). Richer Athenians were afraid of the "naval mob," the poor men who rowed the ships of the navy. They thought the mob could be easily swayed by "clever speakers" and so they used the Council, the 500 men who prepared business for the Assembly, to influence what topics would be discussed in meetings.

Every male citizen had the right to cast his vote at an Assembly where laws were passed (*main picture*). This was democracy – "rule by the people." Juries and officials were paid so that everyone could afford to attend. Even religion was changed so that more people could take part. In the past, the worship of legendary heroes was controlled by a few rich families. Ten new heroes were created so that everyone could claim they had a heroic "ancestor."

○ Hidden History
Can you spot the pizza slice, megaphone, stilts, clock, and notepad? Which don't belong in ancient Athens?

True or False?
Some Athenians were nicknamed "cauliflower ears."

Q3 Why were old pieces of pottery scattered across the ground?

♞ LANGUAGE PUZZLE

Fifth-century-B.C. Athens was a dynamic city that attracted writers and thinkers from all over the Greek world. Three great playwrights, Aeschylus, Sophocles, and Euripides, took the old legends and made them more human, creating the first plays with speaking characters. Aristophanes wrote lively comedies full of people just like his audience. Yet, despite all these new works, Homer remained the most popular author, and

α	β	γ	δ	ε	ζ	η	θ	ι	κ	λ	μ
alpha	beta	gamma	delta	epsilon	zeta	eta	theta	iota	kappa	lambda	mu
a	*b*	*g*	*d*	*e*	*z*	*e*	*th*	*i*	*k*	*l*	*m*

ν	ξ	ο	π	ρ	σ,ς	τ	υ	φ	χ	ψ	ω
nu	xi	omicron	pi	rho	sigma	tau	upsilon	phi	chi	psi	omega
n	*x*	*o*	*p*	*r*	*s*	*t*	*u*	*ph*	*ch*	*ps*	*o*

the language used by the new writers had changed little since the *Iliad*. The Greek alphabet is shown here (*above*) with its modern equivalent. We even get the English word "alphabet" from the first two letters "alpha" and "beta." Can you work out which of the names on the *left* are Achilles, Priam, Odysseus, Agamemnon, and Paris?

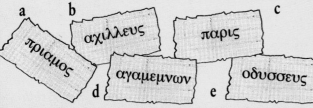

a πριαμος b αχιλλευς c παρις d αγαμεμνων e οδυσσευς

Q2 No. Women, slaves, and "metics" (foreigners living in Athens) were not allowed to vote. Also, some men didn't enjoy going. When an Assembly was held, a gang of slaves walked around with a rope dipped in red paint. Any shirkers who got the paint on them were laughed at and made to pay a fine.

Q3 They were used as voting tablets. If a speaker had too much power over the Assembly, everyone was asked to write down on an *ostrakon*, a piece of broken pottery, the name of anyone they felt had acted wrongly. If at least 6,000 voted, the man with the most votes was banished from Athens for 10 years.

♞ **LANGUAGE PUZZLE ANSWER**
a = Priam, b = Achilles, c = Paris, d = Agamemnon, and e = Odysseus.

○ *Hidden History Answer: Only the megaphone and stilts belong. To find out why, turn to page 29.*

GOING TO MARKET

Hunt the Spy 5
What is an agora?

a spear = spy has bracelets
b market = spy has earrings
c nasty disease = spy has neither bracelets or earrings

When you have all the clues, turn to page 29 to discover who the Spartan spy really is!

Q1 What went on in the market?

Acropolis

Slaves

True or False?
The Athenians loved eating grasshoppers.

🔲 *Hidden History*
Spot the computer, ship, automatic doors, and coffee pot. Which don't belong in the market at ancient Athens?

Q2 What were all the new ideas?

The Oracle Answers

Q1 The first Greek markets were places where farmers swapped goods.

Hidden History Answer: The doors, computer, and coffee pot don't belong. To find out why, turn to page 29.

By the late 6th century B.C., many cities forced people to use their coins. They created large marketplaces, called *agorea* (*main picture*). These were surrounded by buildings where money changers set up their stalls. But a Greek market was also a place where men discussed politics and ideas.

Q2 In the 6th century B.C., philosophers ("lovers of wisdom") began to ask: "Where do we come from?" and "How should we live?" Ordinary Athenians believed these ideas were dangerous – they even executed the philosopher Socrates for corrupting the minds of the young.

After the Persian Wars, the Athenians and other Greek states joined together in a league against Persia. In time, the Athenians', especially under their elected leader, Pericles, forced the smaller states to pay money. This money and the silver from its mines at nearby Laurion allowed Athens to build magnificent temples, many of them on the Acropolis, the high part of the city (*main picture*). The 10,000 slaves working in Athens meant that rich Athenians could live a life of leisure. This gave them time to think about politics, religion, and science. Soon these new ideas were spreading all over Greece.

Q3 What about Greek science?

Q3 Greek scientists made great discoveries in math and medicine. They argued for "laws" that showed logically how the world worked. For example, they said people should be cured by medicine, not magic. They attacked Homer's view that the world was created by gods and there was nothing humans could do to change it.

♞ COUNTING PUZZLE ANSWER
The abacus shows 635, so 311 must have been added.

♞ COUNTING PUZZLE

1
10
100

The ancient Greeks used the abacus as a way of calculating quickly. The beads on each row were moved from left to right. Beads on the top row showed single numbers, the middle row showed tens, and the bottom row hundreds. The abacus (*above left*) shows the number 324. Can you work out what has been added to give the number shown in this abacus (*right*)?

THE PELOPONNESIAN WAR

Q1 What were Greek battles like?

Q2 What happened after the war?

◙ *Hidden History*
Can you spot the balloon, war paint, tomahawk, ghost, and backpack. Which don't belong in an ancient Greek battle?

The Oracle Answers

Q1 Horrible. All Greek armies fought in a similar, brutal way. They marched in columns of hoplites, and when two columns met, they tried to heave each other back using their shields, as only the front line of troops could actually fight. Once a column had forced its way through and broken up the enemy, it was easy to kill opponents as they were no longer protected by their colleague's shields. In Sparta the worst crime a man could commit was to leave the line of battle, because his shield protected the man on his left.

Q2 When the Spartans won, they encouraged the states in the old Athenian Empire to give up

◙ *Hidden History Answer: Only the ghost belongs! To find out why, turn to page 29.*

The rise of the Athenian Empire and the spread of "rule by the people" made other states nervous. Sparta, still the most powerful state on land, decided to attack before Athens became too powerful. In 429 B.C., the Spartans invaded Athenian territory, and 300,000 Athenians crowded into the city for safety. A year later, a terrible plague hit Athens, killing thousands of citizens, including its leader Pericles. The war lasted for 27 years and, for a long time, neither side could gain an advantage. Then Athens lost many of her best soldiers in a disastrous campaign in Sicily. In 402 B.C., the Spartans cut off food supplies to the city, and forced the Athenians to surrender.

SECRET CODE PUZZLE

Greek trickery didn't end with the Trojan horse. The Greeks were great with numbers, and this code system (*below*), written down by Polybius in the 2nd century B.C., was used to convey secret messages. Each letter had a pair of numbers, the horizontal (row) number followed by the vertical (column) number. So the word "No" is 33 34. Can you work out what the message (*below right*) reads?

	1	2	3	4	5
1	A	B	C	D	E
2	F	G	H	I/J	K
3	L	M	N	O	P
4	Q	R	S	T	U
5	V	W	X	Y	Z

43 35 11 42 44 11 33

43 34 31 14 24 15 42 43

52 15 42 15 21 11 32

34 45 43 21 34 42 44

23 15 24 42 31 34 33

22 23 11 24 42.

democracy and return to rule by the rich. But the Spartans could not maintain their strong position, and, for the next fifty years, Greece was divided, as the Spartans, Thebans, and Athenians competed for power.

SECRET CODE PUZZLE

The message reads: "Spartan soldiers were famous for their long hair."

ALEXANDER THE GREAT

The squabbles between Greek city-states in the 4th century B.C. allowed a new power from the north to conquer them all – Macedon. Its king, Alexander the Great, followed in the footsteps of the legendary Agamemnon and led a Greek army into Asia. In a few years, he had defeated the mighty empire of Persia and conquered all the civilizations from the Mediterranean to India.

Alexander (356–323 B.C., *main picture*) made Babylon the capital of his new empire and built many new cities, including Alexandria in Egypt, which became a major center of learning. Alexander possibly died of the disease malaria while still a young man, but his conquests meant that Greek ideas, laws, and customs were spread far and wide.

Never again did the Greeks have so much power. But their language, their art, and their ideas were copied by the Romans and still survive today, in words like "democracy," "history," and "poetry."

Q1 Why was Alexander so great?

The Oracle Answers

Q1 By the age of 33, Alexander had conquered much of the world known to the Greeks. Some historians believe that if he had lived longer, he might have created an empire bigger than Rome. A great general and king, he was taught as a young boy by Aristotle, and had a great interest in Greek ideas and culture. Unlike many Greeks, he wanted to unite his people with the Persians and encouraged his soldiers to marry women from conquered kingdoms. But he was also vain and asked to be worshiped as a god, like the heroes of the Trojan War.

Q2 Because his son was too young to rule, Alexander's generals fought over his conquests. But no single leader emerged, and his empire split into separate kingdoms. In Greece, the city-states continued to fight each other until, divided and weak, they were conquered by Rome in 146 B.C.

True or False?
Ancient Greek vegetarians didn't make sacrifices.

Q2 What happened after Alexander's death?

Hunt the Spy 6
Socrates lived in which Greek city?
a Athens = spy has a beard
b Sparta = spy is bald
c Macedon = spy has no beard and is not bald

Turn to page 29 to discover who the Spartan spy really is!

🔲 **Hidden History**
Can you spot the frisbee, chopsticks, elephant, and chess game? Which belong in Alexander's court?

Q3 What was Alexander's favorite book?

🐴 **THE LEGEND LIVES ON**

The legend of the Trojan Wars didn't die when the Romans conquered Greece. In fact, they were given a new lease of life when the Roman poet Virgil (70–19 B.C.) decided to link the founders of ancient Rome with the Trojan survivors.

In his poem, the *Aeneid*, Virgil described how the Trojan prince Aeneas escaped from the burning Troy, and, after many adventures, arrived in central Italy. Here he married the daughter of the king of the Latins, the future people of Rome. The Roman emperor Augustus claimed he was Aeneas's relative – so the legendary Trojans ended up ruling Rome!

Q3 Alexander loved Homer's *Iliad*, and took a copy everywhere with him. His hero was Achilles, the greatest of the Greek warriors at Troy.

🔲 *Hidden History Answer:*
Only the elephant belongs. To find out the reasons why, turn to page 29.

27

A HOARD OF ANSWERS

HIDDEN HISTORY

Pages 4–5

Merlin was a wizard from Celtic legend. *Dragons* appeared in Greek myths, such as the one that guarded the Golden Fleece. So did *Pegasus* the flying horse, the giant one-eyed *cyclops*, the *Amazon* warrior women, and the goddess *Athena*. In the legend of Troy, Athena helps the Greeks.

Pages 6–7

As *kangaroos* live in Australasia, the Minoans could not have sacrificed them. *Soccer* was first played in China in 100 B.C. (*right*). As in bullfighting, the Cretans killed the bull at the end of the contest, but the *matador* with his red cape dates from Spain in the 1700s. We can be sure the *Minotaur* did not really exist, but it did appear on Cretan coins and paintings.

Pages 8–9

The folding *fan* was invented in Japan in about A.D. 700 (*below*), but, long before, ancient peoples made fans from palm leaves or feathers. The Mycenaeans traded with Africa, and pieces of *ostrich egg* have been found at Mycenae. *Marbles* were played at the time of the Trojan War, according to the Greek historian Athenaeus (A.D. 200). Surprisingly, *pockets* in clothes were a medieval idea. The Maya chewed a type of gum in the 12th century A.D., but *bubblegum* was only invented in the 20th century. Although the Greeks ate a rough kind of *bread*, they never spread *butter* over it as they thought this was only good enough for barbarians. They preferred to use olive oil instead.

Pages 10–11

Windmills were first built in Iran in the 7th century A.D. In the 1st century A.D.,

the Greek inventor Heron designed an early *steam engine* (*right*). Also, the *diolkos*, a paved *track* with two grooves 5ft apart, was built for carts to carry small ships 4 miles across the Isthmus of Corinth (*see map, page 2*). But the Greeks never put the two ideas together! At this time, there were still a few wild *lions* left in Greece. *Barbed wire* was first invented by American Joseph F. Glidden in 1874. Though there weren't really any *sea monsters*, to ancient peoples the deep ocean was a strange place where even whales were like monsters (*below*).

Pages 12–13

Piggyback fights were ancient Olympic events, and flaming *torches* were used for relay races! According to ancient Greek legend, in the Athenian games, a runner's *shorts* slipped down – he tripped over them and was killed. As a result, all Greek athletes competed naked. There were no *referees* showing red cards, but there was a panel of umpires to prevent cheating.

Pages 14–15

Kites were first made in China in the 3rd century B.C., but it is unlikely they would have made their way to Delphi. *Telescopes* were only invented by Dutchman Hans Lippershey in 1608. However, ancient Greek scientists were among the first to study the sun and the stars. *Basketball* was first played in 1891, when American coach James Naismith was asked to create a sport that could be played indoors during winter. Because no boxes were available, he used peach baskets instead, so giving the sport its name! The Greeks had carts but not *baby*

carriages. The *piano* was invented around 1709 by Italian Bartolomeo Cristofori.

Pages 16–17

Spartans were banned from having luxury items like *cakes* and *party dresses*. The Romans used air pressure to create a spray, but the aerosol *spray* was invented in 1926 by Norwegian Erik Rotheim. The *skateboard* was invented by Americans Bill and Mark Richards in 1958. The Greeks didn't have photos, but they did use pinhole *cameras* (*right*). A Greek artist would cover a window with dark material, then punch through a small hole. An upside-down image of the scene outside was seen on the wall and copied.

Pages 18–19

Drums were used for beating time for the rowers. *Whips* weren't used on Greek ships, as the crew were free men. The first *diver* with a helmet and flippers was in 14th-century Germany. However, Alexander the Great was said to have reached the ocean floor in a glass diving bell to talk to the King of Fishes (*page 29, top*).

Hunt the Spy
Now's the time to use your six clues to work out who the Spartan spy is. Perhaps you saw one of these characters (*right*) looking suspicious on pages 14–26? If you can't tell who the spy is from your clues, some of your answers must have been wrong. The answer is on page 32!

Galleons were not built until the 16th century A.D. Most of the oared galleys also had *sails* to help power them.

Pages 20–21

The *pizza* is a modern Italian dish. Actors used masks with mouthpieces like a *megaphone* that helped to project their voices to the audience. The origins of *stilts* are unknown, but the Greeks probably had them. The Greeks didn't have spring-wound *clocks*, but their water clocks let water flow from one bowl into another. When the water stopped flowing, the time was up. The first *notepad* was made in the 1st century A.D. by the Romans from animal skins.

Pages 22–23

The Greeks didn't have *computers*, but in 1947, the "anticythera clock" was discovered. This had interlocking cogwheels which could be used to calculate the positions of the planets, so it was an amazing 2nd-century-B.C. calculator. You might find a *ship* in the agora for the big Athenian festival, the Panathenaia. The Greek inventor Heron used steam power to open *automatic doors,* but not until the 1st century A.D. In legend, *coffee* was found by Ethiopian goat-herds, who noticed their flocks stayed awake all night after feeding on coffee leaves! But it didn't reach Greece until 1500 A.D.

Pages 24–25

The first military *balloons* were made by the Mongols in the 13th century A.D. (*below*). Greek soldiers did not wear *war paint*, but relied on fierce shield and helmet designs to frighten the enemy. The *tomahawk* was a special ax used by the Plains peoples of North America. The Greeks did believe in *ghosts*. Simple *backpacks* (but not the bright-colored modern one on page 25) have been used since ancient times to carry supplies.

Pages 26–27

The first version of *chess* was a Chinese game called "I," which dates from the 4th century B.C. Though Alexander reached India, chess was not played there until the 7th century A.D. The *frisbee* was designed by American Fred Morrison in 1948, and was based on the baking trays of the Frisbie Pie Co.! But the Greek discus (*see* page 18) worked in a similar way! *Chopsticks* were first made in China in the 3rd century B.C. Alexander faced war *elephants* fighting an Indian army at the battle of Hydaspes.

TRUE OR FALSE?

Page 6 *True* – One Minoan sealstone does show especially large Cretan goats used in pairs to pull chariots. **Page 13** *True* – Women could not compete, however, they could win chariot races because the winner was the owner not the rider. **Page 15** *True* – perhaps! Some historians believe the legend of Atlantis may be linked to the island of Thera, which was blown up by a volcano in about 1450 B.C. **Page 17** *True* – A common way for the Spartan army to choose where it was going to camp was to see where a sacred animal sat down. **Page 19** *True* – In 481 B.C. the Persian king Xerxes had the sea whipped for destroying his bridge with a storm! **Page 21** *True* – Athenians who liked the Spartans were called "cauliflower ears," an Athenian joke that the Spartans loved boxing so much they all had extremely damaged ears. **Page 27** *False* – They sacrificed vegetables to the gods instead!

Myth or Reality? Once you have picked out the spy, learn more about the amazing legend of the Trojan horse on pages 30–31.

Scythos the metic   **General Alcibiades**   **Minno the slave**   **Philosopher Hipponax**   **Helen of Lesbos**   **Ibykos the poet**   **Xanthippos the farmer**   **Corinna the fishmonger**   **Sosias the merchant**

THE LEGEND OF THE HORSE

1 THE REAL TROY?

The Troy that the ancient Greeks imagined from Homer's description was a splendid city of wide streets and beautiful temples (*main picture*). Yet none of the nine cities excavated at Troy had the impressive buildings of the legend. In fact, the city that may have been burned to the ground by an invading Greek army, Troy VIIa, covered an area big enough for just 1,000 people to live in – about the same size as the area within the blue walls near "Priam's Palace."

Although we don't know exactly what Troy looked like, there are four buildings hidden in the picture that certainly wouldn't be there. Can you spot them?

Priam's Palace

2 HOMEWARD BOUND

The *Odyssey* tells how it took Odysseus ten years to get home after thinking up the idea of the wooden horse (*see page 4*). Using the maze (*below*), find a route that lets Odysseus (O) reach Penelope (P), his wife, without meeting the one-eyed Cyclops, Circe the witch, the deadly singing Sirens, the whirlpool Charybdis, or the serpent Scylla. Also, Odysseus can't sail past the blue arrows, which are the bad winds sent by Poseidon.

3 THE WOODEN HORSE

Which of these explanations for the wooden horse legend (*see main picture*) is the real one?
• the horse was a kind of battering ram (*below*);
• the horse was a siege tower covered in wet horse hides that protected it against fire arrows;
• the walls were destroyed by an earthquake, and the horse myth started because the symbol for the Greek god of earthquakes, Poseidon, was a horse;
• the real Trojans were horse breeders, so the wooden horse is Homer's joke on them!

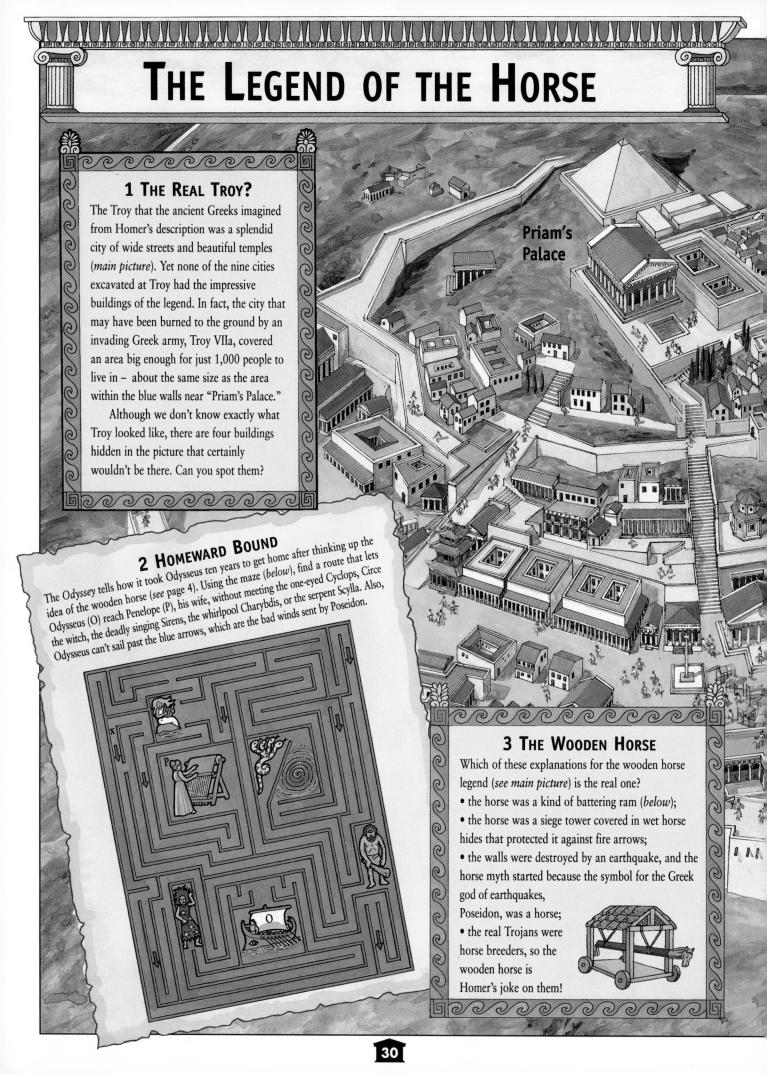

4 ACHILLES' WEAK SPOT

Achilles was the greatest of the Greek heroes at Troy, and Alexander the Great's idol. He is famous for killing the Trojan champion Hector in revenge for the death of his friend Patroclus, then dragging Hector's body three times around the walls of Troy.

According to legend, Achilles' mother, the sea nymph Thetis, dipped him as a baby in the magical Styx River, making him invincible but for one weak spot. Can you guess where this was?

Heart • Heel • Eye • Neck • Buttocks!

5 TREASURE HUNT

Greek legend tells of the fabulous treasures belonging to King Priam of Troy. Look at these objects below. Can you guess which one might be a genuine Trojan treasure?

Vase

Map

Bronze Helmet

Coin

Banquet

Temple of Zeus

6 THE MIGHTY GREEK FLEET

In the *Iliad*, Homer lists the ships taken by each Greek hero to Troy (his total is a huge 1,186). However, the ancient Greeks used letters of the alphabet rather than numbers to count with. So:

$\alpha = 1, \beta = 2\ \gamma = 3, \delta = 4,\ \varepsilon = 5, \zeta = 6, \varsigma = 7, \eta = 8,$
$\theta = 9, \iota = 10, \iota\alpha = 11, \iota\beta = 12, \iota\gamma = 13, \kappa = 20, \lambda = 30, \mu = 40, \mu\varepsilon = 45, \nu = 50, \xi = 60, \xi\eta = 68, o = 70, \pi = 80, \rho = 90, \rho = 100.$

Can you work out how many ships the following kings brought: • Agamemnon = $\rho\theta$ • Ajax = $\lambda\beta$ • Nestor = $\pi\zeta$ • Menelaus = $\xi\varepsilon$ • Odysseus = $\iota\delta$?

Wooden Horse

INDEX

Hunt the Spy
It was General Alcibiades all along. Did you see him lurking in Sparta on page 17? The real Alcibiades was an Athenian general who was accused of offending the gods in Athens during the Peloponnesian War. So he joined the Spartans, telling them all the Athenian secrets. But in the end, tricky Alcibiades died in suspicious circumstances in Asia Minor in 403 B.C.